Published by
Adams Media, a division of F+W Media, Inc.
57 Littlefield Street, Avon, MA 02322. U.S.A.
www.adamsmedia.com

ISBN 10: 1-4405-2801-2
ISBN 13: 978-1-4405-2801-9
eISBN 10: 1-4405-2825-X
eISBN 13: 978-1-4405-2825-5

Printed in the United States of America.

10 9 8 7 6 5 4 3 2 1

Library of Congress Cataloging-in-Publication Data
is available from the publisher.

This publication is designed to provide accurate and authoritative
information with regard to the subject matter covered. It is sold
with the understanding that the publisher is not engaged in
rendering legal, accounting, or other professional advice. If legal
advice or other expert assistance is required, the services of a
competent professional person should be sought.
—From a *Declaration of Principles* jointly adopted
by a Committee of the American Bar Association
and a Committee of Publishers and Associations

Many of the designations used by manufacturers and sellers to
distinguish their product are claimed as trademarks. Where
those designations appear in this book and Adams Media was
aware of a trademark claim, the designations have been printed
with initial capital letters.

Interior illustration © clipart.com

*This book is available at quantity discounts for bulk purchases.
For information, please call 1-800-289-0963.*

An Introduction to

Greed

greed
(greed)
NOUN: Excessive desire, especially for wealth or
possessions.

The seductive lure of avarice has left a bitter taste
on the tongues of many: Midas quickly learns to rue
his golden touch. King Ahab's love of excess earns
him a vineyard, but costs him his beloved Jezebel.
And Macbeth's lust for power leads him to regicide.
The aching desire for more has led to the downfall
of many an upright man, but the ways in which this
sin reveals itself are abundant. The myriad dimen-
sions of acquisitiveness, the most rapacious of sins,
can be difficult to comprehend, but this dictionary
of indulgence is your key to defining greed—in all its
manifestations.

A

❧

abduct
(ab-DUKT)
VERB: To take a person away secretly and illegally, often by use of force; to kidnap.

abscond
(ab-SKOND)
VERB: To depart quickly and in secret, especially to avoid criminal charges. To *abscond* is to secretly flee the consequences of one's acts, particularly those acts leading to illicit gain.

accept
(ak-SEPT)
VERB: To take into possession.

accrete
(uh-KREET)
VERB: To accumulate or cause to become attached.

ache for
(AYK fohr)
VERB: A strong desire for something or someone.

acquire
(uh-KWYR)
VERB: To obtain something; to come into possession.

acquisitive

(uh-KWIZ-it-iv)

ADJECTIVE: A greedy tendency to acquire money or material things.

> *The king's ACQUISITIVE nature required rooms upon rooms in the castle to be dedicated to the storage and display of his many treasures.*

ad infinitum

(ad ihn-fi-NY-tuhm)

ADJECTIVE: Without end; literally, "to infinity." The phrase refers to things without end or to something that is limitless. In practical use, *ad infinitum* usually carries a sense of ironic overstatement.

addiction

(uh-DICKT-shunn)

NOUN: The state of being psychologically dependent on something or someone.

adopt

(uh-DOPT)

VERB: To accept or take as one's own.

affluenza

(a-floo-EN-zuh)
NOUN: A word combining affluent and influenza, *affluenza* has come to stand for a disease that affects wealthy young people who have suddenly come into large sums of money.

amass

(uh-MASS)
VERB: To collect or gather quantities of materials or things over time.

amoral

(ay-MOR-uhl)
ADJECTIVE: Without moral discretion or standards. To be *amoral* is to act as though the distinctions of right and wrong are nonexistent. A person who is *amoral* is neither moral nor immoral.

annihilate

(uh-NY-uh-layt)
VERB: To completely destroy.

appetence

(AP-eh-tents)
NOUN: Intense longing or desire; a natural craving.

appetency
(AP-eh-ten-see)
NOUN: Strong, unwavering desire.

> *One can tell Sandra has an APPETENCE for the finer things in life as she instinctively selects the most expensive wares without even looking at the price.*

appetite
(ap-eh-TYT)
NOUN: The desire to satisfy a bodily need or craving, such as for food. Also, the desire for something non-food-related, such as power or sex.

appetition
(ap-eh-TISH-in)
NOUN: A medical term meaning a desire for, longing for, or seeking after something.

appraise
(uh-PRAYZ)
VERB: To estimate (an item's) value.

appropriate
(uh-PRO-pree-ayt)
VERB: To take something without permission; to steal.

Earth provides enough to

satisfy every man's need, but

not every man's greed.

—MAHATMA GANDHI

arrogate
(AYR-uh-gayt)
VERB: To demand something for oneself or to take control without authority.

aspire
(uh-SPYR)
VERB: To hope to achieve something; to be eagerly desirous.

> *The ambitious statesman ASPIRES to climb the chain of power, but his motivation is not to better the lives of his constituents; his only focus is personal gain.*

athirst
(uh-THERST)
ADJECTIVE: Thirsty or eager for something.

attachment
(uh-TATCH-ment)
NOUN: Affection or regard for someone or something; the feeling that binds the two together.

audacious
(aw-DAY-shuss)
ADJECTIVE: Brazen, daring, or fearless. *Audacious* refers to bold, unrestrained, uncompromising behavior.

augment

(awg-MEHNT)

VERB: To make bigger; increase; enhance.

augmentation

(awg-mehn-TAY-shun)

NOUN: The process of increasing in extent, size, or scope. The broadening, extension, or increase of something is that thing's *augmentation*.

auxiliary

(awg-ZIL-yuh-ree)

NOUN: Backup, reserve, extra.

avarice

(AV-er-iss)

NOUN: Great desire for riches. *Avarice* is extreme greed.

> *The Pharaoh's AVARICE resulted in the constant raids and looting of neighboring kingdoms.*

avaricious

(av-uh-RISH-us)

ADJECTIVE: Showing great desire for riches or extreme greed for wealth.

avidity

(uh-VID-ih-tee)

NOUN: Greediness, eagerness.

B

bamboozle
(bam-BOO-zuhl)
VERB: To deceive; to trick.

batten
(BAT-un)
VERB: To feed greedily or to fatten.

begrudge
(bee-GRUHJ)
VERB: To give or grant reluctantly.

begrudgingly
(bee-GRUHJ-ing-lee)
ADVERB: To do something in a begrudging manner; to give something in a reluctant way.

belly-guts
(BELL-ee-guhts)
NOUN: A slang term for someone who is greedy and lazy.

belt
(belt)
VERB: In addition to being something that needs loosening when one has eaten too much, as a verb *belt* means to drink quickly or greedily.

bequeath

(bee-KWEETH)

VERB: Bestow by means of a will. *Bequeath* is often used metaphorically to describe something handed down to a group of people from those of a past era.

Even though the family members could not stand the sight of each another, they all gathered at their great-uncle's manor to see whom he BEQUEATHED his fortune to after his passing.

beseech

(bih-SEETCH)

VERB: To entreat, implore, or request earnestly. *Beseech* is a formal verb used to request something. In contemporary use, it reflects either great (or even fawning) politeness or urgency of the highest order.

besiege

(bih-SEEJ)

VERB: To submit a person or body to insistent demands from all sides; to crowd around; to harass.

bestow

(bih-STOW)

VERB: To confer or give. One *bestows* an award, honor, or degree. The verb is usually followed by *on* or *upon*.

Who covets more is

evermore a slave.

—ROBERT HERRICK

big eyes
(big ayes)
NOUN, IDIOM: A greedy or covetous look.

bilk
(bihlk)
VERB: To swindle or cheat. Someone who defrauds a person or institution of funds or goods *bilks* the victim.

> *Elizabeth's plan to BILK the orphanage of its funds was foiled when the charity's board followed the twisted paper trail she left.*

binge
(bihnj)
VERB OR NOUN: As a verb, to indulge in excess, especially in food or alcohol; as a noun, a period of time spent indulging.

binger
(BIHNJ-er)
NOUN: A person who binges.

blackmail
(BLAK-mayl)
VERB: Extortion of payment through threats of revelation.

blandish
(BLAN-dihsh)
VERB: To coax someone to do something for you through the use of flattery. You might also hear the noun form of this word, which is *blandishment*.

bogart
(BO-gahrt)
VERB: To selfishly take or keep something, often in reference to a marijuana joint.

bolt
(bohlt)
VERB: To eat extremely quickly.

bottomless pit
(BAW-tuhm-less piht)
NOUN, IDIOM: Insatiable, usually in reference to hunger for food.

bribable
(BRY-buh-buhl)
ADJECTIVE: Easily bribed.

bribe

(bryb)

VERB OR NOUN: As a verb, this means to convince someone to do something or give something in exchange for a gift or money. As a noun, it refers to the gift or money given in exchange for services or objects.

bribery

(BRY-bur-ee)

NOUN: The act of giving or offering a bribe.

burn for

(bern fohr)

VERB, IDIOM: To want or desire something intensely.

buzzard

(BUH-zerd)

NOUN: A grasping, avaricious person.

Jeremy was such a BUZZARD, the second Jacob was dead he started rifling through his belongings.

C

cache

(kash)

NOUN: A place where things of value are hidden; also, the things stored there.

cacoethes

(kak-oh-EE-theez)

NOUN: Frenzied desire, especially for something harmful; uncontrollable urgency.

> *Once she understood how the wagers worked, Lily couldn't quell her CACOETHES for gambling her savings away.*

capitalize

(KA-pih-tuh-lyz)

VERB: To draw an advantage from. Also, in business terms, *capitalize* can mean funding a business or converting a business's value to personal income.

carousal

(kuh-ROWZ-ul)

NOUN: Revelry. Noisy and lively, often associated with eating or drinking to excess.

carouse

(kuh-ROWZ)

VERB: To engage in boisterous social activity or to drink to excess.

carte blanche
(kawrt blonsh)
NOUN: Unrestricted power, access, or privilege; permission to act entirely as one wishes. *Carte blanche* is from the French for "blank document"; the essential meaning is that one is free to "write one's own ticket."

cheat
(cheet)
VERB OR NOUN: As a verb, acting dishonestly or unfairly. As a noun, a person who acts dishonestly or unfairly.

cheese-paring
(CHEEZ-payr-ing)
ADJECTIVE: While you might expect this to mean finding a wine that pairs perfectly with that aged Cheddar, it actually means stingy or economical with money.

choke down
(chohk down)
VERB: To force yourself to eat something.

chow
(chow)
VERB: To eat heartily.

clandestine

(klan-DESS-tihn)

ADJECTIVE: Kept hidden; secreted away from authorities or public observance. A *clandestine* object is one that is concealed for a purpose hidden from general view.

> *The pair's secret trysts started as a way to satisfy their lustful urges but developed into CLANDESTINE meetings where the two planned out how they were going to extort money from Eleanor's husband.*

clingy

(KLING-ee)

ADJECTIVE: Holding onto; not easily separated.

close-fisted

(kloss-fihst-id)

ADJECTIVE: Stingy with money.

clutch

(klutch)

VERB OR NOUN: As a verb, to hold something tightly and firmly or to seize or snatch. As a noun, a small purse.

Greed is an imperfection
that defiles the mind; hate
is an imperfection that
defiles the mind; delusion
is an imperfection that
defiles the mind.

—Siddhārtha Gautama

coffers
(KAW-fers)
NOUN: A treasury, a place in which money is kept or stored.

collateral
(kuh-LAT-uh-ruhl)
NOUN OR ADJECTIVE: As a noun, something pledged as security or insurance for the fulfillment of an obligation or payment. As an adjective, secondary or accompanying.

comp
(kawmp)
VERB: Short for compensate.

compensate
(KAWM-pun-sayt)
VERB: Giving something in return for or to make up for services performed, or for something lost; giving something in exchange.

complimentary
(kawm-pluh-MEN-tuh-ree)
ADJECTIVE: Expressing praise or admiration; also, extended without charge.

con out

(kawn owt)

VERB: To use deception in order to procure something that one desires.

conatus

(koh-NAY-tuss)

NOUN: Natural impulse.

> *While the man understood that his fellow castaways faced the same hunger pains and starvation, his CONATUS to survive caused him to steal the little food the group had collected.*

concupiscence

(kawn-KYU-puh-senss)

NOUN: Sexual lust or longing.

concupiscent

(kawn-KYU-puh-sent)

ADJECTIVE: Marked by strong desire, especially strong sexual desire.

confiscate

(KAWN-fiss-kayt)

VERB: To deprive of (one's property), especially as part of an official or governmental body.

congest
(kuhn-JEST)
VERB: To clog or fill to excess.

conspiracy
(kuhn-SPEER-uh-see)
NOUN: A treacherous plan involving two or more persons.

consume
(kuhn-SOOM)
VERB: To eat or drink.

consumerism
(kuhn-SOO-mer-iz-uhm)
NOUN: A society's preoccupation with materialism and the acquisition of goods.

consumption
(kuhn-SUHMP-shunn)
NOUN: The act of eating or drinking.

contrivance
(kuhn-TRY-vuhnss)
NOUN: A device or artful means of acquiring or performing something. *Contrivance* may refer to an actual mechanical object or, more darkly, to a plot or scheme.

copious

(KO-pee-uss)

ADJECTIVE: Abundant; large or generous in extent. That which is broad in scope or abundant is *copious.*

cormorant

(KOR-mer-uhnt)

NOUN: Someone who is excessively grasping or insatiably greedy.

> *Forget holiday bonuses, the factory owner was such a CORMORANT that he forced his workers to come in on Christmas Day.*

cornucopia

(kohr-nuh-COE-pee-uh)

NOUN: This Latin word means "horn of plenty," and a *cornucopia* has become a familiar symbol of Thanksgiving: a hornlike container overflowing with nature's bounty. In general, a *cornucopia* is an overabundance, a seemingly inexhaustible supply of something.

corpulence

(KOHRP-yew-lenss)

NOUN: The state of being obese or fat.

corpulent
(KOHRP-yew-luhnt)
ADJECTIVE: Obese; fat; bulky.

corrupt
(kuh-RUHPT)
ADJECTIVE: Achieving personal gain from an act of dishonesty or deceit.

cotton to
(KAW-tun too)
VERB: To be fond of or like something.

covet
(KUHV-iht)
VERB: To yearn for or desire something or someone.

> *The man could not resist COVETING his neighbor's many goods despite everything he was taught in catechism.*

covetous
(KUHV-ih-tuss)
ADJECTIVE: Greedy and willing to go to shameless lengths to earn wealth.

covetousness
(KUHV-ih-tuss-ness)
NOUN: The act of being greedy and shameless.

cozen
(KUHZ-uhn)
VERB: To trick or to obtain through deception.

cram
(kram)
VERB: To fill or stuff to overflowing.

crapulent
(KRAP-yuh-lunt)
ADJECTIVE: Relating to eating or drinking (often alcohol) in excess.

crapulous
(KRAP-yuh-luss)
ADJECTIVE: From the Latin meaning "sick with gluttony," *crapulous* describes someone who eats and drinks too much, or it describes the effects of eating and drinking too much.

crave
(krayv)
VERB: A powerful desire or yearning for something or someone.

craver
(KRAY-ver)
NOUN: A person who longs or desires.

craving
(KRAY-ving)
NOUN: An intense desire or yearning.

crib
(krihb)
VERB: To steal or take without permission; sometimes refers to another person's work or writing.

crook
(krook)
NOUN: A person who is dishonest or steals.

crooked
(KROOK-ihd)
ADJECTIVE: Dishonest.

cull
(kuhl)
VERB: To assemble or collect bit by bit; to select.

cupidity
(kyew-PIHD-uh-tee)
NOUN: Greed; extreme desire for wealth. One who is obsessed with acquiring money shows *cupidity*.

curmudgeon
(ker-MUDJ-in)
NOUN: A close-minded miser.

> *Charles Dickens created the quintessential CURMUDGEON in Ebenezer Scrooge, only to have the old miser break from his avaricious ways after his night with the three spirits.*

D

debauchery

(dih-BOTCH-er-ee)

NOUN: Licentiousness; overindulgent sexual expression. To accuse someone of *debauchery* is to say that person is intemperate and immoral with regard to indulgence in physical pleasures.

decadence

(DEK-uh-dunss)

NOUN: Characterized by declining moral standards. *Decadence* can refer to the declining standards of a nation, a period of time, or an individual.

defalcate

(dih-FOWL-kayt)

VERB: To embezzle.

> *He was able to DEFALCATE more than double his salary from the company by falsifying a few documents.*

demand

(dee-MAND)

VERB: Insist urgently.

demolish

(dih-MAWL-ish)

VERB: To destroy or devour completely.

deplete
(dih-PLEET)
VERB: To use up completely; to exhaust.

deserve
(dih-ZERV)
VERB: To be worthy of or qualified for something.

desiderate
(dih-SID-uh-rayt)
VERB: To desire or wish for something.

desideratum
(dih-sid-uh-RAY-tum)
NOUN: A thing to be desired. *Desideratum* finds its plural in *desiderata*, which is also the name of a popular short writing that outlines worthy spiritual objectives.

desire
(dih-ZYR)
VERB OR NOUN: As a verb, to want or crave. As a noun, a longing or feeling of wanting.

desirous
(dih-ZY-russ)
ADJECTIVE: Characterized by desire.

devour
(dih-VOWR)
VERB: To eat or consume quickly, voraciously, and entirely.

devouringly
(dih-VOWR-ing-lee)
ADVERB: To do in a devouring manner.

diddle
(DIHD-uhl)
VERB: To cheat or swindle.

dipsomaniacal
(dihp-soh-muh-NYE-uh-kuhl)
ADJECTIVE: *Dipsomania* is an uncontrolled craving for alcohol, so someone who suffers from this craving is considered *dipsomaniacal*.

> *Her husband's alcoholism stole more from her family than their savings as his selfish, DIPSOMANIACAL behavior also robbed their children of a father.*

dog-eat-dog
(dawg-eet-dawg)
ADJECTIVE: Competitive, willing to use force or violence to win.

He who buys what he does

not need steals from himself.

—AUTHOR UNKNOWN

drool
(drool)
VERB: Drip saliva from the mouth; also, make an excessive show of pleasure.

dupe
(doop)
VERB OR NOUN: As a verb, to fool, trick, or deceive. As a noun, a person so deceived.

> *Lex felt guilty that the con required him to DUPE a priest, but he did not think he would be able to find another DUPE so trusting to take the fall.*

duplicity
(doo-PLISS-uh-tee)
VERB: Trickery; two-facedness; purposeful deceptiveness.

dying (for)
(DY-ing fohr)
VERB: An informal way of saying that one is extremely desirous of something.

E

There is a very fine line

between loving life and

being greedy for it.

—MAYA ANGELOU

eager

(EE-ger)

ADJECTIVE: Having keen desire; wanting something very much.

eagerness

(EE-ger-ness)

NOUN: The state of being eager.

edacious

(ih-DAY-shuss)

ADJECTIVE: Given to eating; devouring.

> *The EDACIOUS young boy began to grow in size even faster once he started stealing food off his brothers' and sisters' plates.*

edacity

(ih-DASS-ih-tee)

NOUN: The state of being edacious.

embezzle

(ihm-BEZZ-ul)

VERB: To appropriate funds for oneself that were placed in one's care for another party.

empty

(EMP-tee)

ADJECTIVE: Hungry.

englut
(ehn-GLUHT)
VERB: Gulp down; satiate.

engorge
(ehn-GORJ)
VERB: Eat or swallow in excess.

engulf
(ehn-GUHLF)
VERB: To swallow up or to eat whole.

entice
(ehn-TYSS)
VERB: To tempt in a pleasing fashion; to attract or lure.

envelop
(ehn-VELL-uhp)
VERB: Completely surround something or someone.

> *The overpowering corporation ENVELOPED the small, independently run stores that could not compete against its deep pockets.*

envy
(EHNN-vee)
NOUN OR VERB: A strong desire for something, and unhappiness that one does not have it.

esurience

(ih-SHOOR-ee-inss)

NOUN: The state of being esurient.

esurient

(ih-SHOOR-ee-uhnt)

ADJECTIVE: Greedy; hungry.

exact

(ihg-ZAKT)

VERB: Obtain from someone through demands.

exceed

(ehk-SEED)

VERB: Go beyond the normal size, amount, or number.

excess

(EHK-sess)

NOUN: An amount than is more than necessary; too much.

excessive

(ehk-SESS-iv)

ADJECTIVE: Beyond the normal amount; something characterized by excess.

exorbitant

(ihg-ZOHR-bih-tuhnt)

ADJECTIVE: Too high or expensive; excessive.

> *The boutique's EXORBITANT prices allow only the wealthiest to shop there.*

exorbitantly

(ihg-ZOHR-bih-tuhnt-lee)

ADVERB: Beyond what is reasonable; extreme or excessive.

exploit

(ehk-SPLOYT)

VERB: Benefit or advance oneself through the work of others.

exploitation

(ehk-sploy-TAY-shun)

NOUN: The use of something for profit, especially if the profit-making does not benefit the person or thing being used.

extort

(ehk-STOHRT)

VERB: To obtain by force or threats.

extortionate

(ehk-STOHR-shun-it)

ADJECTIVE: Another word for *exorbitant*, meaning too much or too high.

extra

(EHK-struh)

ADJECTIVE: More than the original amount; additional.

extract

(ehk-STRAKT)

VERB: Remove, get, or draw out with force or effort.

eyes for

(ayes fohr)

NOUN, IDIOM: To want nothing but that person or thing.

F

famished
(FAM-isht)
ADJECTIVE: Extremely hungry.

fancy
(FAN-see)
VERB: Having a desire or liking for something.

fastidious
(fuh-STIHD-ee-uss)
ADJECTIVE: Attentive to detail or issues of propriety; hard to please. A *fastidious* person is meticulous, exacting, and sensitive to procedure.

> *Thomas was FASTIDIOUS about his finances, always knowing where every penny was kept and spent.*

Faustian
(FOWS-tee-un)
ADJECTIVE: Faust is the antihero of a German legend who sold his soul to the devil in order to gain great knowledge. Thus, *Faustian* describes the sacrificing of moral or spiritual values in order to gain knowledge, fame, money, etc.

feast
(feest)
VERB: To eat sumptuously.

Be glad that you're greedy;

the national economy would

collapse if you weren't.

—Mignon McLaughlin

felonious

(fuh-LOHN-ee-uss)

ADJECTIVE: Criminal; villainous; reminiscent of or relating to a felony crime.

fervor

(FER-ver)

NOUN: Passionate feeling.

filch

(filch)

VERB: To steal, especially to steal petty amounts or inexpensive goods.

> *That little boy just attempted to FILCH that elderly woman's purse right out of her hand! Right here on the street!*

fleece

(fleess)

VERB: To swindle someone out of money, as with a hoax.

flimflam

(FLIM-flam)

NOUN: A swindle.
VERB: To swindle.

forage
(FOHR-ihj)
VERB: To search or hunt for food and provisions.

forcible
(FOHRSS-uh-buhl)
ADJECTIVE: Powerful; using force to achieve a goal.

fraud
(frawd)
NOUN: Deception for profit; trickery, deceit.

freebooter
(FREE-boo-ter)
NOUN: A pirate; one who takes his loot—or booty—without asking.

frenzy
(FREHN-zee)
NOUN: A state of wild excitement; extreme emotional or mental agitation.

fresser
(freh-ser)
NOUN: A Yiddish slang term for a glutton.

G

gain
(gayn)
VERB: To acquire an addition; to obtain something desired.

galore
(guh-LOHR)
ADJECTIVE: In abundance; plentiful.

gannet
(GAN-iht)
NOUN: A British slang term for a greedy person or heavy eater.

garbage disposal
(GAHR-bij dis-POHZ-uhl)
NOUN: A slang term for a person who will eat or consume almost anything.

garner
(GAWR-ner)
VERB: To amass, gather, or accumulate. To *garner* something is to acquire it over a period of time.

> *According to his father, Zion would GARNER more wealth if he invested in a solid portfolio.*

Greed is a bottomless pit

which exhausts the person

in an endless effort to

satisfy the need without ever

reaching satisfaction.

—ERICH FROMM

gasþ (for, after)
(gasp fohr)
VERB: Crave; eagerly desire.

get
(geht)
VERB: To receive something or have something come into one's possession.

gild
(gild)
VERB: To cover thinly with gold; also, to make something appear more valuable or appealing than it actually is.

gimmes
(GIMM-eez)
NOUN: Slang term for "give-mes," meaning a state of wanting.

give eyeteeth for
(gihv aye-teeth fohr)
VERBAL IDIOM: To give something that one values in order to gain something that one desires.

glean

(gleen)

VERB: To collect; to gain bit by bit; to obtain one piece or morsel at a time.

> *The farmer did not want to lose any piece of grain during the harvest, so he had his farmhands follow the mechanical reaper and GLEAN every last bit.*

glom

(glawm)

VERB: To look at with rapt attention or to steal something. "*Glom* onto" means to take possession of something, such as someone else's ideas.

glut

(gluht)

VERB OR NOUN: As a noun, an abundant supply. As a verb, to fill to satiety.

glutton

(GLUHT-uhn)

NOUN: A person who eats excessively and greedily.

gluttony

(GLUHT-un-ee)

NOUN: Excessive eating.

gobble
(GAWB-uhl)
VERB: To swallow or eat hurriedly and hungrily.

gobble-guts
(GAWB-uhl guht)
NOUN: A term from the early seventeenth century meaning glutton.

gorb
(gorb)
NOUN: An Irish slang term meaning glutton.

gorge
(gohrj)
VERB: To stuff oneself greedily with food.

gorger
(GOHR-jur)
NOUN: A person who is known to eat greedily and in excess.

gormandize
(GOHR-mun-dyz)
VERB: To eat in a greedy, ravenous manner. Someone who *gormandizes* eats to satisfy a voracious appetite. This type of eater is known as a gourmand and is very different from a gourmet, who is someone who cultivates refined tastes for food of the finest quantity.

gormandizer

(GOHR-muhn-dyz-er)

NOUN: A person who tends to gormandize or eat greedily.

gouge

(gowj)

VERB: To rip someone off or swindle.

gourmand

(goor-MAWND)

NOUN: One who eats well and to excess.

Emily is a true GOURMAND and will spare no expense on ingredients, purchasing truffles, saffron, and all the other finest ingredients.

grab

(grab)

VERB: To grasp or take something with force; to obtain quickly.

grabalicious

(gra-buh-lish-uss)

ADJECTIVE: A slang term meaning greedy, covetous.

grasþing
(GRASS-ping)
ADJECTIVE: Desiring the possessions of others, often through illegal or unethical means.

grasþingness
(GRASS-ping-ness)
NOUN: The act of greedily desiring what others have.

gratis
(GRAT-iss)
ADJECTIVE: Free of charge.

> *Liza has more money than she knows what to do with, but still expects GRATIS gifts from her favorite designers.*

greed
(greed)
NOUN: Excessive desire for something, especially wealth or power. One of the seven deadly sins.

greedhead
(GREED-hehd)
NOUN: An avaricious person.

greediness
(GREE-dee-ness)
NOUN: The act of being greedy. Showing desirous, selfish wanting.

greedy
(GREE-dee)
ADJECTIVE: Having or showing greed. Intense wanting, selfish desire.

greedy-guts
(GREE-dee guhts)
NOUN: A slang term for someone who is being greedy or acting like a glutton.

grifter
(GRIHF-tur)
NOUN: A person who engages in unseemly activities; a swindler, a dishonest gambler, etc.

gully-gut
(GUH-lee guht)
NOUN: A slang term meaning a glutton.

gulp
(guhlp)
VERB: Swallow eagerly and quickly, in large amounts.

gut-ache
(GUHT-ayk)
NOUN: A slang name for someone who is greedy.

guttie
(GUH-tee)
NOUN: A slang term for a glutton.

guttle
(GUH-tuhl)
VERB: Eat with greed and enjoyment.

> *The corpulent duke GUTTLED the entire feast without throwing a single morsel to his starving servants.*

guzzle
(GUHZ-uhl)
VERB: To eat or drink greedily.

guzzled
(GUHZ-uhld)
ADJECTIVE: Slang term meaning drunk; having drunk in excess.

guzzle-guts
(GUHZ-uhl guhts)
NOUN: A slang term for a drunkard or a greedy person.

gyp
(jihp)
VERB: Cheat or swindle.

H

Calm self-confidence is as

far from conceit as the desire

to earn a decent living is

remote from greed.

—Channing Pollock

haggle
(HAG-ul)

VERB: To bargain with; to dicker or negotiate on price or terms.

> *She is so tightfisted with her money that she tries to HAGGLE the price on every purchase she makes.*

hanker
(HAYN-ker)

VERB: Desire eagerly.

hankering
(HAYN-ker-ing)

NOUN: A craving.

harpy
(HAWR-pee)

NOUN: An extremely greedy person.

hearty
(HAWR-tee)

ADJECTIVE: *Hearty* is a word that wears many hats. From warm-hearted to violent, it can also mean robust when referring to an appetite.

hedonism
(HEE-duhn-ihz-uhm)

NOUN: The pursuit of pleasure and gratification.

hedonist

(HEE-duh-nihst)

NOUN: One whose life is devoted solely or primarily to the pursuit of pleasure and gratification.

hoard

(hohrd)

VERB: To accumulate and hide or store away for future use.

hoarder

(HOHR-der)

NOUN: A person who hoards things.

hog

(hawg)

NOUN OR VERB: As a noun, a *hog* is someone who greedily keeps or takes things. As a verb, to *hog* means the act of keeping or taking things.

hogging

(HAW-gihng)

VERB: To keep all of something for oneself.

hoggish

(HAW-gihsh)

ADJECTIVE: Gluttonous, greedy.

hoodwink

(HOOD-wingk)

VERB: Deceive or trick someone.

hoover

(HOO-ver)

VERB: To consume greedily. See *vacuum*.

hornswoggle

(HORN-swah-guhl)

VERB: To cheat or deceive someone.

> *Do not play cards with Richard. He'd HORNSWOGGLE his own father to win the pot.*

hose

(hohz)

VERB: To cheat or screw someone; to take advantage.

houndish

(HOWN-dihsh)

ADJECTIVE: A slang term for shamelessly gluttonous.

hunger

(HUHN-gur)

NOUN: A desire or craving.

hunger (for or after)

(HUHN-ger fohr or af-ter)

VERB: Have a strong desire for something.

> *In order to satisfy her HUNGER to rule the most expansive kingdom imaginable, the rapacious queen sent her armies east and west to conquer and colonize.*

hungriness

(HUHN-gree-ness)

NOUN: The state of being hungry.

I

idolatry

(aye-DAWL-uh-tree)

NOUN: The worship of a physical object as though it were a god or idol; to display an unusual and worshipful attachment to an object.

imbibe

(ihm-BYB)

VERB: To drink. *Imbibe* is generally used to describe the drinking of alcoholic beverages, though it can also carry the meaning "to take in (an idea)."

immeasurable

(ih-MEZH-er-uh-buhl)

ADJECTIVE: Describes a quantity that cannot be measured because it seems to be limitless.

incessant

(ihn-SESS-uhnt)

ADJECTIVE: Continuous. *Incessant* derives from the Latin roots for "without end."

indulge

(ihn-DUHLJ)

VERB: Allowing oneself to yield to the pleasure of something.

indulgence
(ihn-DUHL-jentz)
NOUN: The act of indulging or the thing that is indulged in.

infatuated
(ihn-FATCH-yew-ayt-ed)
ADJECTIVE: Absorbed by an unreasoning attraction.

infatuation
(ihn-fatch-yew-AY-shun)
NOUN: The act of being infatuated.

ingrate
(IHN-grayt)
NOUN: An ungrateful person. A person who does not show the proper respect or gratitude toward someone who has provided help might be called an *ingrate*.

> *Penelope learned that money cannot buy manners when she came to realize how much of an INGRATE the wealthy Samuel was; after everything she did for him, he was completely unappreciative.*

ingurgitate
(ihn-GUHR-juh-tayt)
VERB: To swallow greedily.

Even in a time of elephantine

vanity and greed, one never

has to look far to see the

campfires of gentle people.

—GARRISON KEILLOR

inhale

(ihn-HAYL)
VERB: To eat greedily and quickly.

inordinate

(ihn-OR-duhn-it)
ADJECTIVE: Excessive; too much.

insatiability

(ihn- say-shuh- BIHLL-uh-tee)
NOUN: The inability to satisfy a desire or appetite.

insatiable

(ihn-SAY-shuh-buhl)
ADJECTIVE: Incapable of satisfaction; not satiable.

insidious

(ihn-SIHD-ee-uss)
ADJECTIVE: Designed to entrap; happening or
spreading harmfully but subtly; stealthily and
seductively treacherous.

> *The sensual temptress was an excellent swindler; with
> her INSIDIOUS tactics, the unsuspecting men willingly
> gave her what she asked.*

intemperance

(ihn-TEM-per-uhns)
NOUN: Excessive appetite; a lack of self-control.

intemperate

(ihn-TEM-per-iht)

ADJECTIVE: Lacking self-control; indulgent to the extreme.

Daniel's privileged, without-bounds upbringing has left him unruly and INTEMPERATE, overspending and overindulging whenever he feels like it.

itch

(itch)

VERB: A strong desire.

A greedy person and a

pauper are practically one

and the same.

—SWISS PROVERB

jealous

(JEHL-uhss)

ADJECTIVE: Showing or feeling envy towards someone.

jones (for)

(johnz fohr)

VERB: To have a craving for something.

Spending the weekend at his brother-in-law's estate left William JONESING for a lifestyle that was far beyond his means.

K

keep
(keep)
VERB: To retain or hold something.

kill
(kihl)
VERB: To finish something completely.

> *Even though she was the hostess, Gretta greedily KILLED the last of the champagne, without offering any to her guests.*

knock back
(nawk bak)
VERB: To drink or eat quickly.

The curse of the romantic

is a greed for dreams, an

intensity of expectation

that, in the end, diminishes

the reality.

—MARYA MANNES

L

languish (for or after)

(LANG-gwish)

VERB: To pine for someone or something.

lascivious

(luh-SIHV-ee-us)

ADJECTIVE: Wanton or lustful. That which excites sexual desires is lascivious.

lecherous

(LETCH-er-uhss)

ADJECTIVE: Excessive desire; lustful in a suggestive, potentially offensive way.

The LECHEROUS baron expected everything to be his, including any woman he laid his eyes on.

lechery

(LETCH-er-ee)

NOUN: Lustfulness; excessive sexual indulgence.

liberate

(LIHB-uh-rayt)

VERB: While the term *liberate* has positive meanings, such as to set someone free, it also informally means to steal.

Covetous persons are like

sponges which greedily drink

in water, but return very little

until they are squeezed.

—G. S. Bowles

lickerish
(LIHCK-er-ish)
ADJECTIVE: Another word for *lecherous*. Greedy, lustful.

long (for)
(lawng fohr)
VERB: To have a desire or wish.

longing
(LAWNG-ing)
NOUN: Yearning; a strong craving.

loot
(loot)
NOUN OR VERB: As a verb, to steal. As a noun, the object or bounty that has been stolen.

lucre
(LOO-ker)
NOUN: Profits; financial rewards; money.

> *After the bank heist, the robbers returned to their hideout to count and divide the resulting LUCRE.*

lust
(luhst)
NOUN OR VERB: As a noun, strong desire. As a verb, to have strong desire or yearning.

luxuriate
(luhg-ZHOOR-ee-ayt)
VERB: Indulge or enjoy oneself.

M

Three great forces rule

the world: stupidity,

fear, and greed.

—Albert Einstein

Mammon
(MAM-uhn)
NOUN: Wealth regarded as evil; sometimes the personification of greed.

mania
(MAY-nee-uh)
NOUN: Excessive enthusiasm or excitement.

> *She had a certain MANIA when it came to her many belongings; she expected everything to be in a certain place.*

manipulate
(muh-NIP-yuh-layt)
VERB: To control or manage in a way that may be unfair or unscrupulous.

material
(muh-TEER-ee-uhl)
NOUN: Physical substance; essence; something from which things are or can be constituted.

materialism
(muh-TEER-ee-uh-liz-uhm)
NOUN: The valuing of material objects or money higher than spiritual or cultural matters.

materialistic

(muh-teer-ee-uh-LISS-tik)

ADJECTIVE: A way of describing someone who places material wealth above spiritual wealth.

megalomania

(mehg-uh-loh-MAY-nee-uh)

NOUN: Delusions of wealth and/or power. Literally, *megalomania* is a psychopathological condition in which a person is obsessed with fantasies of riches or authority.

Although Lucy was of average wealth and social status, her MEGALOMANIA often had her living much beyond her means.

mercenariness

(muhr-suhn-AYR-ee-ness)

NOUN: The state of being mercenary.

mercenary

(MUHR-suhn-ayr-ee)

ADJECTIVE: Doing something only for money or for reward, without regard to ethics.

milk

(mihlk)

VERB: In addition to being a nutritious beverage, *milk* as a verb can mean to get everything one can from a person or from circumstances.

mingy
(MIHN-jee)
ADJECTIVE: Stingy and mean.

misappropriate
(miss-uh-PROH-pree-ayt)
VERB: To dishonestly take something, such as funds.

miser
(MYE-zer)
NOUN: A person who is stingy or greedy with money and spends as little of it as possible.

miserly
(MY-zer-lee)
ADJECTIVE: Like a miser, being stingy with money.

money
(MUHN-ee)
NOUN: A form of currency; bills and coins.

moneybags
(MUHN-ee-bagz)
NOUN: A wealthy person.

money grab
(MUHN-ee grab)
NOUN: The acquisition of a large amount of money in an undignified way.

money-grubber
(MUHN-ee gruhb-er)
NOUN: A person who is overeager to make money.

money-hungry
(MUHN-ee-hun-gree)
ADJECTIVE: Extreme greed for money.

motivation
(moh-tuh-VAY-shun)
NOUN: The reason for doing something or behaving in a certain way.

mug
(muhg)
VERB: To rob someone.

mulct
(muhlkt)
VERB: To obtain something by swindling a person.

With the time and effort it takes him to MULCT funds from the unsuspecting, he could be earning double doing honest work.

N

The ignorant mind, with its

infinite afflictions, passions,

and evils, is rooted in the

three poisons. Greed, anger,

and delusion.

—BODHIDHARMA

narcissism

(NAHR-suh-sihz-uhm)

NOUN: Excessive fascination with oneself; greediness and selfishness are likely characteristics as well.

need

(need)

VERB: To require something.

It truly amazes the billionaire's servants that no matter how much wealth he amasses, he still NEEDS so much from them.

nick

(nihk)

VERB: A British term meaning to steal or take.

niggardly

(NIG-erd-lee)

ADJECTIVE: Stingy; unwilling to give, share, or spend.

nouveau riche

(noo-voh-REESH)

NOUN OR ADJECTIVE: As a noun, a recently wealthy person. As an adjective, having recently become wealthy. *Nouveau riche* is often used to describe those whose newfound wealth brings with it a tact-less or overbearing attitude.

You know how showy the NOUVEAU RICHE are—we that come from money choose to invest it more wisely.

nympholepsy
(NIHM-foh-lehp-see)

NOUN: Frenzied desire for something unattainable.

O

Nothing makes us more

vulnerable than loneliness,

except greed.

—Thomas Harris

obese
(oh-BEESS)
ADJECTIVE: Grossly overweight.

obtain
(ub-TAYN)
VERB: To get or acquire.

omnivorous
(awm-NIHV-er-uss)
ADJECTIVE: Accustomed to eating both animal and vegetable food items. *Omnivorous* (derived from the Latin word for "eating everything") can also mean "voracious" in the sense of taking all that is offered.

opulent
(AWP-yew-lent)
ADJECTIVE: Rich; characterized by wealth or extravagance.

> *The lavish gala was held in a manor on a hill, full of OPULENT furniture and décor.*

overeat
(oh-ver-EET)
VERB: To eat too much.

overeater

(oh-ver-EET-er)

NOUN: A person who eats too much.

overindulge

(oh-ver-ihn-DULJ)

VERB: To indulge and have too much of something.

> *The spread of cookies and cakes and fancy desserts was meant for the entire party; however, the greedy little boy chose to eat more than the rest and OVERINDULGED on the sweets.*

overindulgence

(oh-ver-ihn-DULJ-ence)

NOUN: The act of overindulging.

P

pack (away)
(pak a-WAY)
VERB: To eat or drink a large quantity of something.

pant (for)
(pant fohr)
VERB: Long for someone or something.

parlay
(PAWR-lay)
VERB: To take something—such as talent or a small amount of money—and attempt to use it to gain great fortune or success.

> *Our new plan for wealth is to PARLAY our son's deformity into riches via the circus scene.*

parsimonious
(pawr-suh-MOHN-ee-uss)
ADJECTIVE: Stingy; exceptionally frugal or thrifty.

partake
(pawr-TAYK)
VERB: To participate and share in.

We are all born brave,

trusting, and greedy, and

most of us remain greedy.

—Mignon McLaughlin

peckish
(PEHK-ish)
ADJECTIVE: Hungry.

peculate
(PEHK-yew-layt)
VERB: To steal something, such as public funds, that has been entrusted to one's care.

> *Many were disappointed when they heard Valencia planned to PECULATE the school's charitable donations because she seemed like such a trustworthy teacher.*

penny-pinching
(PEHN-ee PIHN-ching)
ADJECTIVE: Miserly and stingy with money.

penurious
(peh-NOOR-ee-uss)
ADJECTIVE: Miserly. *Penurious* can also mean destitute or extremely poor.

pig out
(pihg owt)
VERB: To eat to excess.

piggish
(PIHG-ish)
ADJECTIVE: Greedy and gluttonous, like a pig.

pilfer
(PIHL-fer)
VERB: To take without authorization or permission; to steal.

pillage
(PIHL-ihj)
VERB: Rob or strip of goods, often using violence.

pinch
(pihnch)
VERB: To steal.

pinch-fart
(pihnch-fahrt)
NOUN: A slang term for a miser.

pinch-fist
(pihnch-fihst)
NOUN: A slang term for a miser.

pine (for)
(pyn fohr)
VERB: Desire strongly and eagerly.

pirate
(PY-ruht)
NOUN OR VERB: In addition to being a person who commits illegal acts at sea, as a verb *pirate* means to use or reproduce without permission for profit.

> *Rather than leave a map with an X to mark the spot, the old PIRATE chose to keep the location of his buried treasure a secret—if he could not enjoy his spoils, no one would.*

plenitude
(PLEHN-ih-tood)
NOUN: Abundance. *Plenitude* is the standard spelling; *plentitude*, though commonly used, is generally considered incorrect.

pleonectic
(plee-oh-NEHK-tihk)
ADJECTIVE: Covetous or greedy.

pleonexia
(plee-uh-NEHK-see-uh)
NOUN: Insatiable greed.

plethora
(PLEHTH-er-uh)
NOUN: Excessive oversupply. To have a *plethora* of something is to have a vast quantity of it.

plunder
(PLUHN-der)
VERB: To take with force, especially during wartime.

poach
(pohch)
VERB: In addition to being a healthy way to cook eggs, *poach* means to take in an unfair way.

polish off
(PAWL-ish awf)
VERB: To finish something entirely, sometimes quickly.

polyphagia
(paw-lee-FAY-jee-uh)
NOUN: A medical term meaning excessive eating (*poly* means "excessive" and *phagia* means "the eating of a specified substance").

pork out
(pohrk OWT)
VERB: Stuff oneself with food.

possess
(puh-ZEHSS)
VERB: Own; have as a belonging.

possession
(puh-ZESH-uhn)
NOUN: The state of ownership.

possessive
(poh-ZESS-ihv)
ADJECTIVE: Unwilling to share; desirous to own and keep things.

> *Nathaniel's greed went beyond material things, as he was very POSSESSIVE of his wife's time, expecting her to always be at his beck and call.*

power
(POW-er)
NOUN: Ability to influence or have command over others.

predatory
(PREHD-uh-tohr-ee)
ADJECTIVE: Exploiting others; literally preying on someone.

prehensile
(pree-HEHN-suhl)
ADJECTIVE: Grasping, greedy, avaricious. An animal can have a *prehensile* limb or tail, meaning capable of grasping.

procure
(proh-KYEWR)
VERB: To obtain. Someone who *procures* something gathers or collects it.

prodigal
(PRAWD-ih-guhl)
ADJECTIVE: Extravagant or wasteful; imprudent.

profusion
(proh-FYEW-zhun)
NOUN: An abundance or extravagance.

purloin
(PER-loyn)
VERB: To steal or to take by dishonest means.

put away
(put uh-WAY)
VERB: To eat or drink in large quantities.

Greed, like the love of

comfort, is a kind of fear.

—Cyril Connolly

quaff

(kwaff)

VERB: Drink heartily, especially alcohol.

quid pro quo

(kwihd proh KWOH)

NOUN: A thing given in return for something else;
Latin: "something for something."

*Nothing is ever a generous favor with Roger, who
operates QUID PRO QUO. Whenever he does anything
for you, he expects something in return.*

R

ram

(ram)

VERB: To cram or stuff forcefully, firmly.

rampage

(RAM-payj)

NOUN: An instance reminiscent of frenzied violence; a destructive period of self-indulgent behavior.

rapacious

(ruh-PAY-shuss)

ADJECTIVE: Given to plunder or the forcible overpowering of another. *Rapacious* is related to the word rape.

rapacity

(ruh-PASS-uh-tee)

NOUN: The state of being rapacious.

> *The RAPACITY of modern civilization knows no bounds, as people are willing to rape the land for personal gain.*

raven

(RAV-ihn)

VERB: Devour voraciously.

We tend to forget that

happiness doesn't come as a

result of getting something

we don't have, but rather of

recognizing and appreciating

what we do have.

—FREDERICK KEONIG

ravenous

(RAV-uh-nuss)

ADJECTIVE: Powerfully hungry. *Ravenous* can also mean intensely eager to be satisfied.

ravenousness

(RAV-uh-nuss-ness)

NOUN: The state of being ravenous.

ravin

(RAV-in)

NOUN: Plunder; seizure of property.

> *When the McDougals ran out of money, the landowner claimed their cottage as RAVIN and took the rent out of their belongings.*

reap

(reep)

VERB: To gather or take in, as profits or a crop.

relentless

(rih-LEHNT-lehss)

ADJECTIVE: Unceasingly harsh; unyieldingly intense or severe.

relish
(REHL-ihsh)
VERB: To enjoy heartily; also, an instance of great enjoyment.

require
(ree-KWYR)
VERB: To need something or someone.

revel in
(REHV-uhl ihn)
VERB: To luxuriate or take pleasure in; to indulge in boisterous activity.

rip-off
(rihp-awff)
NOUN: Something overpriced; also a fraud.

robber
(RAWB-er)
NOUN: A person who steals or commits a robbery.

robbery
(RAWB-er-ee)
NOUN: The action of taking or stealing personal property.

S

sate

(sayt)

VERB: To satisfy completely or to excess.

satiate

(SAY-shee-ayt)

VERB: Satisfy beyond reasonable expectation. To be *satiated* is to consume to excess.

satisfy

(SAT-ihs-fye)

VERB: To fulfill desires, expectations, or needs.

> *Never one to worry about others, Vincent made sure to SATISFY his own thirst before offering any water to those with whom he was traveling.*

scam

(skam)

VERB: Deceiving people out of money or valuables; swindle.

scarf

(skahrf)

VERB: To eat voraciously or enthusiastically.

scavenge
(SKAV-ihnj)
VERB: To search for and gather or collect, often from discarded waste.

scoff (down)
(skawf down)
VERB: To eat greedily.

score
(skohr)
VERB: To achieve something.

screw
(skrew)
VERB: *Screw* has two greedy meanings: one is to cheat or swindle someone (as in "you got *screwed*") and the other is to extort money from someone (as in "she just *screwed* money out of him").

scrooge
(skrewj)
NOUN: A miserly person who acts like Ebenezer Scrooge, the main character in Dickens's *A Christmas Carol*.

A greedy father has

thieves for children.

—SERBIAN PROVERB

secure
(sih-KYEWR)
VERB: *Secure* is a word that wears many adjectival and verbal hats, from describing a feeling of contentedness to directing the fastening of doors. As a verb, it also means to succeed in obtaining something.

seize
(seez)
VERB: To take hold with force; to capture or confiscate.

> *Andrew did not hesitate to SEIZE control of his father's company when he grew ill.*

self-indulgence
(SELF-ihn-DUHL-jenss)
NOUN: The quality of indulging in one's own interests or desires without restraint.

selfish
(SEHL-fihsh)
ADJECTIVE: Looking out for one's own interests, regardless of the needs of others.

sharking
(SHAHR-kihng)
ADJECTIVE: Gluttonous, greedy.

shoplift

(SHAWP-lihft)

VERB: To steal merchandise from a store.

shovel

(SHUHV-uhl)

VERB: In addition to being a tool for picking up snow, *shovel* means to stuff or push quickly, as with food.

shylock

(SHY-lawk)

NOUN: From the character in Shakespeare's *Merchant of Venice*, a *shylock* is a moneylender who heartlessly charges excessive interest rates.

sigh for

(sye fohr)

VERB: Desire keenly.

simony

(SYE-muh-nee)

NOUN: The sin of buying or selling ecclesiastical privileges or benefices.

sinesthesia

(sihn-ehss-THEE-zhuh)

NOUN: A slang term meaning committing all seven deadly sins at once (pride, envy, greed, lust, anger, gluttony, and sloth).

skim

(skihm)

VERB: Remove something off of the top; embezzle or steal small amounts at a time.

skinflint

(SKIHN-flihnt)

NOUN: A miser; someone who does not enjoy spending his or her money.

The man who is a SKINFLINT will have his savings enjoyed by those who inherit them.

slake

(slayk)

VERB: To quench one's thirst or satisfy a need or craving.

snaffle

(SNAFF-uhl)

VERB: To take something without permission.

sordid
(SOHR-dihd)
ADJECTIVE: Tawdry. That which is base or undignified is *sordid*.

spoil
(spoyl)
VERB OR NOUN: As a verb, to rob someone or take by force. As a noun, the goods taken.

spoil for
(spoyl fohr)
VERB: To be extremely eager for something or someone.

sponge
(spuhnj)
NOUN: A mechanism that readily accepts liquid; also, a person who consumes lots of liquid, such as alcohol.

sponge off
(spuhnj awf)
VERB: Obtaining money or food without doing or paying anything in return.

status

(STAT-uss)

NOUN: Social ranking or classification.

After coming into a large sum of money, the couple was more excited over their new STATUS than their ability to provide for their family.

steal

(steel)

VERB: To take something from another person, sometimes with force or in secret.

stiff

(stihf)

VERB: To cheat someone out of money.

stingy

(STIHN-jee)

ADJECTIVE: Not generous; unwilling to part with money.

stive

(styv)

VERB: To stuff or fill; to stifle.

stodge

(stawj)

VERB: A slang term meaning to eat to excess.

stuff
(stuhf)
VERB: To fill tightly or cram, especially with food.

stuffed
(stuhfd)
NOUN: The state of having eaten too much.

suck down
(suhk down)
VERB: To eat or drink something greedily.

sucked dry
(suhkd dry)
VERB: To exhaust resources.

superfluous
(soo-PER-floo-uhss)
ADJECTIVE: Unnecessary. That which exceeds what is essential is *superfluous*.

surfeit
(SER-fiht)
NOUN OR VERB: As a noun, excess. As a verb, to have too much of something.

suspire

(suh-SPYR)

VERB: To breathe in a longing, sighing manner.

swallow

(SWAWL-oh)

VERB: To allow something to pass from the mouth into the throat and down into the stomach.

Walter's plan was to marry Jennifer, SWALLOW her assets, and then divorce her.

sweet tooth

(SWEET tooth)

NOUN: A desire for sweet, sugary foods.

swindle

(SWIHN-dul)

VERB: To cheat someone out of money or other possessions.

That deceitful conman did not think twice about SWINDLING the elderly couple out of their money.

swinish

(SWY-nihsh)

ADJECTIVE: See *hoggish*.

swipe

(swyp)

VERB: To steal or take.

T

take

(tayk)

VERB: To get into one's control or possession; to seize or capture.

tenacious

(tuh-NAY-shuss)

ADJECTIVE: Not easily separated; not wanting to let go of a possession.

> *She was TENACIOUS about keeping her mother's locket because she knew her sister wanted it as well.*

theft

(thehft)

NOUN: The act of stealing or committing a crime.

thief

(theef)

NOUN: A person who steals or commits theft.

thirst

(therst)

NOUN: The state of needing liquid; also, a strong desire or craving.

Lust and greed are more

gullible than innocence.

—MASON COOLEY

thrust
(thruhst)
VERB: Push suddenly or violently.

tick
(tihk)
NOUN: In addition to being a blood-sucking arachnid, *tick* is a slang term for a greedy, selfish person.

tightfisted
(tyt-FIHS-tihd)
ADJECTIVE: Miserly and stingy with money.

> *Your brother is TIGHTFISTED; I asked him to help us pay for your father's funeral and he refused.*

tightwad
(TYT-wawd)
NOUN: A stingy, mean, or miserly person.

U

unending
(uhn-EHN-dihng)
ADJECTIVE: Without termination or close; continuing forever.

unquenchable
(uhn-KWEN-chuh-buhl)
ADJECTIVE: Not able to be satisfied.

unremitting
(uhn-ruh-MIHT-ing)
ADJECTIVE: Persistent; relentless.

Initially, she refused to go on a date with him, but after his UNREMITTING attempts at asking her, she finally said yes.

unrestrained
(uhn-rih-STRAYND)
ADJECTIVE: Not controlled or restrained.

urge
(erj)
NOUN: An impulse or strong desire.

It is preoccupation with

possessions, more than

anything else, that prevents us

from living freely and nobly.

—THOREAU

usurious

(yew-ZHER-ee-uhss)
NOUN: Charging excessive interest on money loaned; characterized by usury.

usurp

(yew-SERP)
VERB: To assume forcibly and/or without right. To *usurp* is to take over.

> *It was always Benjamin's plan to USURP leadership of the commune, and once Alan was sick, he took his opportunity.*

usury

(YEW-zher-ee)
NOUN: Excessive interest on a loan. Someone who demands extravagant payment in exchange for money lent out practices *usury*.

V

It is greed to do all the

talking but not to want to

listen at all.

—Democritus

vacuum

(VAK-yewm)

VERB: In addition to being a household cleaning appliance, *vacuum* as a verb can mean to greedily and quickly consume something.

venal

(VEE-nul)

ADJECTIVE: Corruptible or excessively devoted to selfish interests (as opposed to public interests); susceptible to bribes.

> *The mayor himself was not evil; however, he was so VENAL that any evil entity could easily swoop in and work his puppet-strings.*

voracious

(voh-RAY-shuss)

ADJECTIVE: Greedily hungry. Someone who is gluttonous or ravenous is *voracious*.

voraciousness

(voh-RAY-shuhss-nehss)

NOUN: The state of being voracious.

voracity

(voh-RASS-uh-tee)

NOUN: The state of being voracious or greedily hungry.

vulturous

(VUHL-cher-uhs)

ADJECTIVE: A term to describe the type of person who preys on others, as a vulture might prey on sick or injured animals.

With the thought of inheritance at the forefront of his mind, the VULTUROUS grandson began visiting his grandmother much more frequently the sicker she became.

Hell has three gates:

lust, anger, and greed.

—BHAGAVAD-GITA

wangle
(WANG-guhl)
VERB: To get one's own way by using manipulation or clever means.

want
(wahnt)
VERB: Desire, wish, crave.

> *It was hard to tell what was greater—the old miser's wealth or his WANT for more.*

wealth
(wehlth)
NOUN: An abundant amount of money or valuable possessions or property; an abundance of anything.

welsh
(wehlsh)
VERB: To fail to honor or fulfill a debt or obligation.

win
(wihn)
VERB: To be victorious.

wish
(wihsh)
VERB: To long for; desire; want.

wolf
(woolf)
VERB: To devour greedily.

wolfish
(WOOLF-ish)
ADJECTIVE: To act greedily or in a devouring manner.

wrest
(rehst)
VERB: To take away; to pull away forcefully.

> *Andrew wanted all the toys in the children's playroom for himself so he WRESTED Julianna's favorite doll from her hands, leaving his young sister in tears.*

Y

The love of money is

the root of all evil.

—Proverb

yearn
(yern)
VERB: A strong longing for something.

yearning
(YER-ning)
NOUN: To yearn or long for something or someone.

> *His girlfriend's intense YEARNING to be by his side at all times was once romantic, but now he realizes this emotional want commands all of his attention.*

yen
(yehn)
NOUN: A desire, craving, or longing for something or someone.

Z

Greed is a fat demon with a

small mouth and whatever

you feed it is never enough.

—Janwillem van de Wetering

zeal

(zeel)

NOUN: Fervor and enthusiasm for someone or something; ardor.

zero in

(ZEE-roh ihn)

VERB: To set one's sights on something.

> *Michael would not be happy until all of his competition was eliminated, so he ZEROED IN on destroying David's company and taking his business.*